Alfred's Premier Piano Course

Dennis Alexander • Gayle Kowalchyk • E. L. Lancaster • Victoria McArthur • Martha Mier

Alfred's *Premier Piano Course* Performance Book 5 includes motivational music in a variety of styles, reinforcing concepts introduced in the Lesson Book 5.

The pieces in this book correlate page by page with the materials in Lesson Book 5. They should be assigned according to the instructions in the upper right corner of selected pages of this book. They also may be assigned as review material at any time after the student has passed the designated Lesson Book page.

A compact disc recording is included with this book. It can serve as a *performance* model or as a *practice* companion. See information about the CD on page 32.

Performance skills and musical understanding are enhanced through *Premier Performer* suggestions. Students will enjoy performing these pieces for family and friends in a formal recital or on special occasions. See the List of Compositions on page 32.

D1367220

Edited by Morton Manus

Cover Design by Ted Engelbart
Interior Design by Tom Gerou
Illustrations by Jimmy Holder
Music Engraving by Linda Lusk

ISBN-10: 0-7390-6009-0
ISBN-13: 978-0-7390-6009-4

Use with Alfred's Premier Piano Course,
Lesson Book 5, pages 4–5

Rhythm Workout

On your lap, tap the rhythm 3 times daily
as you count aloud.

Count: 1 e + a 2 e + a

Caprice*

CD 1/2 GM 1

Allegro

* *Caprice* is a French word that describes pieces in a light-hearted mood,
with sudden and impulsive changes in the music.

Premier Performer *Perform Caprice in a playful, humorous manner.*

Missouri River Ballad

CD 3/4 GM 2

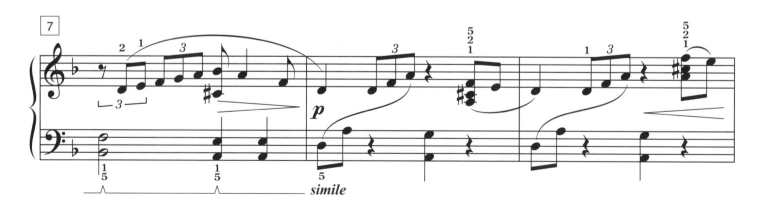

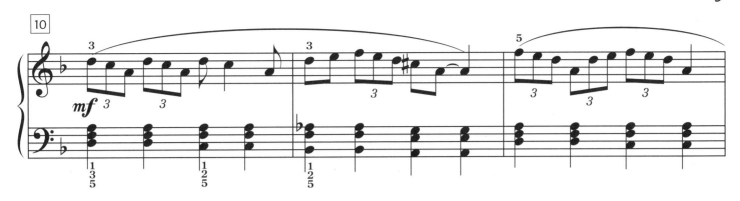

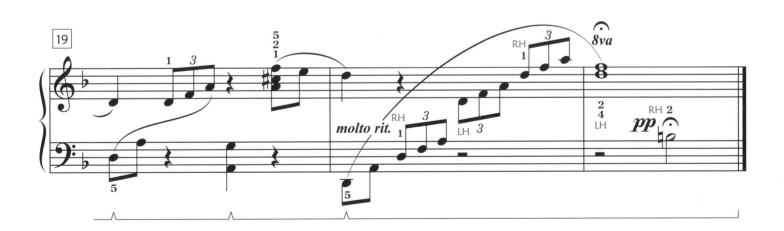

Premier Performer *Play very expressively with much attention to dynamics and tempo markings.*

A Splash of Indigo

CD 5/6 GM 3

Rhythm Workout

On your lap, tap the rhythm 3 times daily as you count aloud.

$\frac{3}{8}$

Count: 1 + 2 + 3 + 1 + 2 + 3 +

Moderate jazz waltz tempo

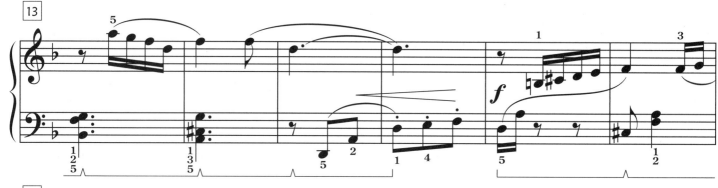

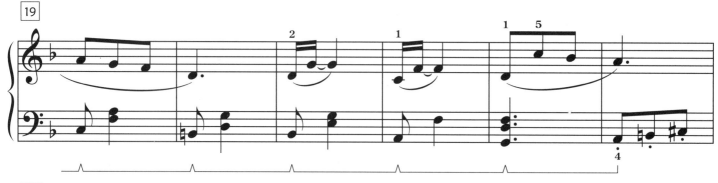

> **Domenico Scarlatti** *(1685–1757) was an important Italian composer born in the same year as Johann Sebastian Bach. He was one of 10 children of the famous composer, Alessandro Scarlatti. Domenico worked for both the royal families of Portugal and Spain. His approximately 550 keyboard sonatas, written for harpsichord, often imitate the sounds of Spanish guitars.*

Minuetto
Second Movement
from *Sonata in C Major*

CD 7/8 GM 4

Domenico Scarlatti
K. 73b: L. 217

Section A

Moderato

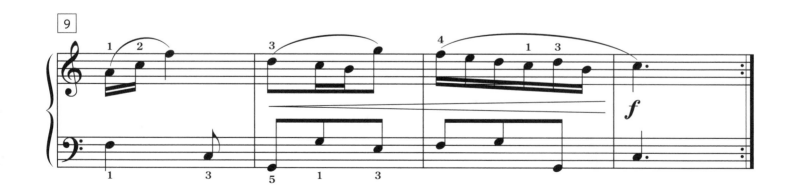

Section B

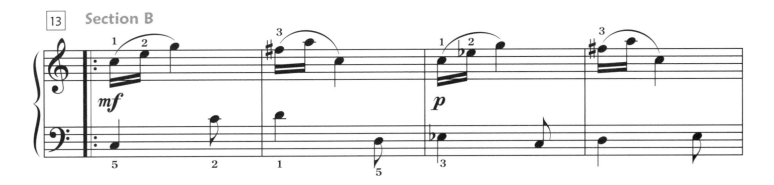

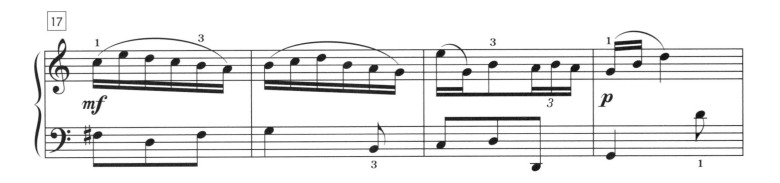

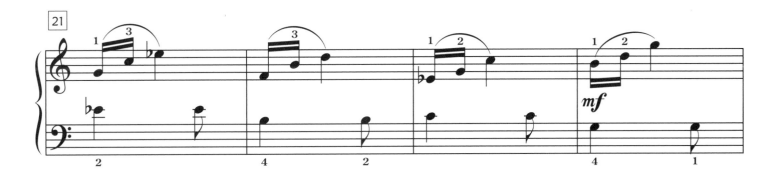

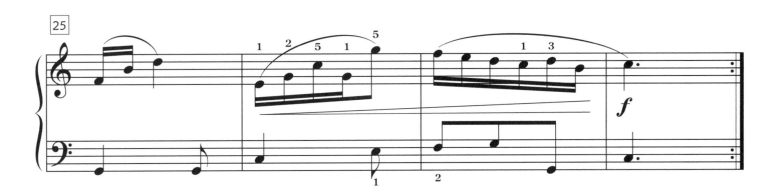

Premier Performer

Slightly emphasize the first note of each measure to make the piece sound dance-like. This emphasis should be subtle.

Watercolor Impressions

CD 9/10 GM 5

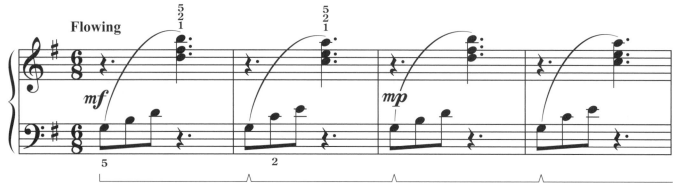

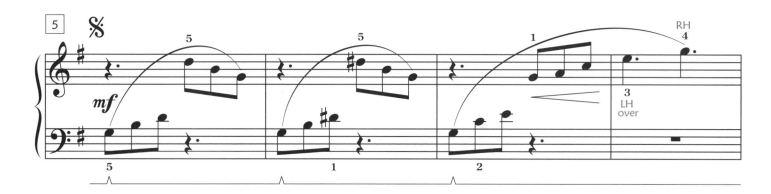

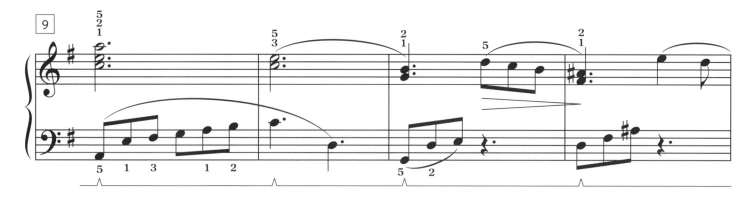

The Fifers

CD 11/12 GM 6

> **Jean-François Dandrieu** (1682–1738) was a French composer who lived during the Baroque period. When he was five, he played his first harpsichord concert for the king of France, Louis XIV. The title, The Fifers, refers to musicians who played a small flute-like instrument called the fife. High in pitch, it was mainly used in military bands. It has since been replaced by the piccolo.

Look at the key signature
and name the key. _____ major

Jean-François Dandrieu

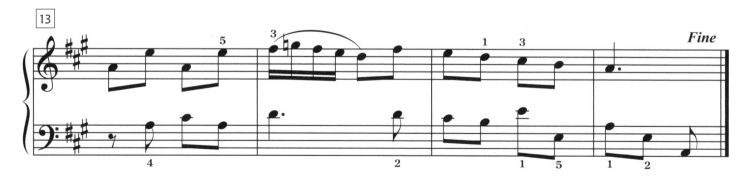

* Play all eighth notes slightly detached.

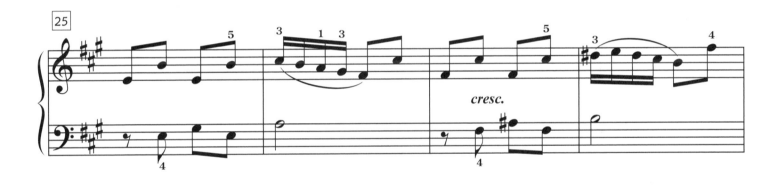

Premier Performer *Make each voice distinct by following the articulation markings carefully.*

German Dance in ___ Major*

CD 13/14 GM 7

A **German Dance** is a couple's dance from late 18th- and early 19th-century Europe. Usually written in $\frac{3}{4}$ or $\frac{3}{8}$ time, it evolved into the waltz and ländler. Like the Haydn German Dance on this page, most German dances are written in major keys and have two sections—each eight measures in length. Other composers who wrote German dances include Mozart, Beethoven and Schubert.

Franz Joseph Haydn
(1732–1809)

* Look at the key signature and name the key.

Little Etude in ___ Major*

CD 15/16 GM 8

* Look at the key signature and name the key.

Lesson Book: pages 28–29

Robert Schumann (1810–1856) was one of the most important German composers of the 19th century. Although Schumann dreamed of becoming a concert pianist, he injured his hand. After that, he turned his full attention to composing. Schumann married his piano teacher's daughter, Clara, the first highly regarded female concert pianist. She helped spread Schumann's fame, playing his works across Europe.

Soldier's March
from Album for the Young

CD 17/18 GM 9

Robert Schumann
Op. 68, No. 2

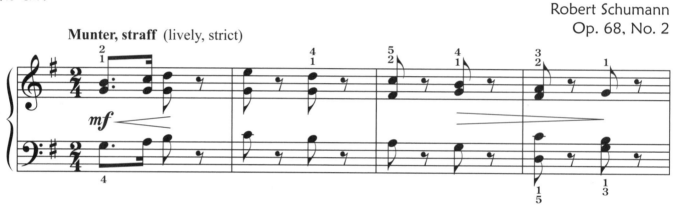

Premier Performer *Shape the phrases by following the dynamics.*

> ***Muzio Clementi*** *(1752–1832) was born in Italy but lived much of his life in England. He is considered to be the first composer to write specifically for the piano. He had a varied and successful career that included being a performer, conductor, piano manufacturer, music publisher, and editor of Beethoven's music. Clementi's most famous composition is his Sonatina in C Major, Op. 36, No. 1.*

Sonatina in C Major
(Second Movement)

Muzio Clementi
Op. 36, No. 1

CD 19/20 GM 10

(Pedal is optional.)

* ***tr*** is a symbol for trill. Play this ornament using the suggestion given in the small notes above the symbol.

Premier Performer *Listen for beautiful singing lines in the RH melody and keep the LH soft and delicate throughout.*

Sonatina in C Major
(Third Movement)

CD 21/22 GM 11

Muzio Clementi (1752–1832)
Op. 36, No. 1

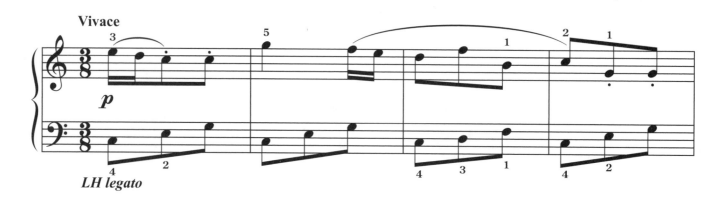

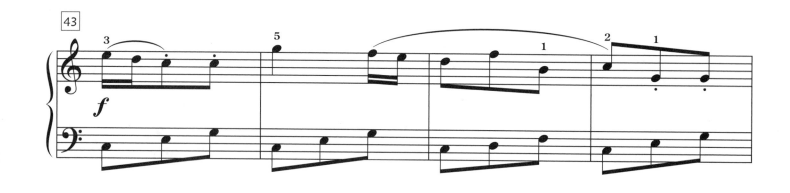

Lesson Book: pages 34–35

Blues Toccata

CD 23/24 GM 12

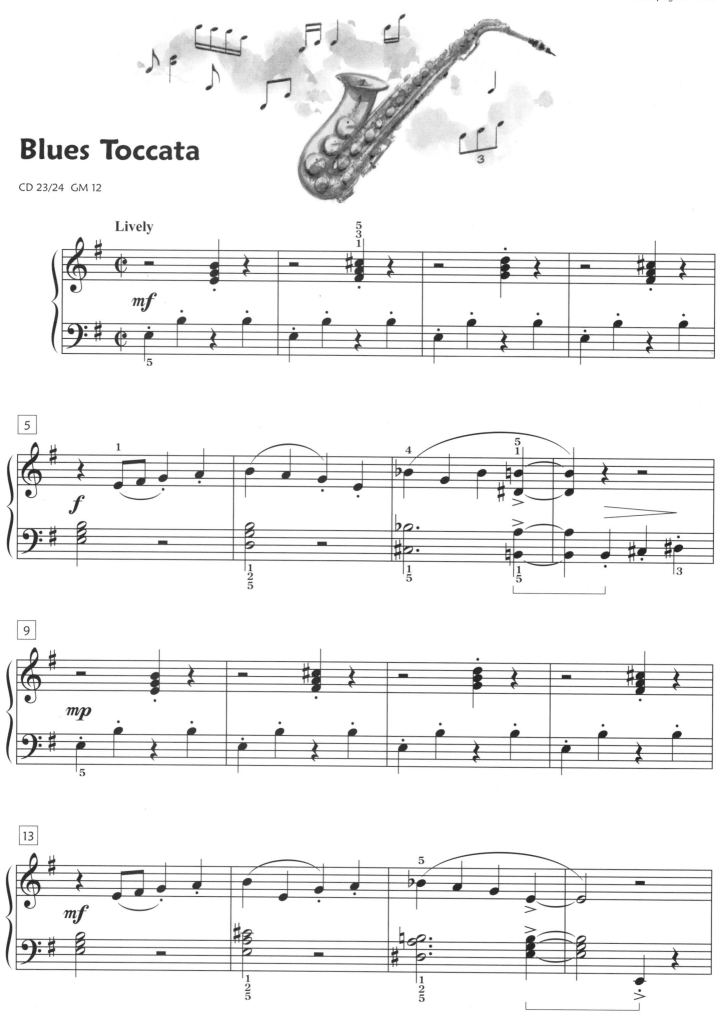

Premier Performer *Feel two beats per measure as you perform.*

Climbing the Pyrenees*

CD 25/26 GM 13

* The Pyrenees Mountains form the border between France and Spain.

Premier Performer

Maintain firm fingertips and a rounded hand position to play all sixteenth notes evenly.

Lesson Book: pages 42–43

June: Barcarolle

from *The Seasons*

CD 27/28 GM 14

Peter Ilych Tchaikovsky
Op. 37b, No. 6

> **Peter Ilych Tchaikovsky** (1840–1893) was a Russian composer of the Romantic era. He had a troubled life, but one that produced some of the most beautiful melodies ever written, including those found in the Swan Lake and Nutcracker ballets. The Seasons consists of 12 short character pieces for piano, one for each month of the year. "Barcarolle" was written for the sixth month, June, and is reminiscent of a trip to the seashore.

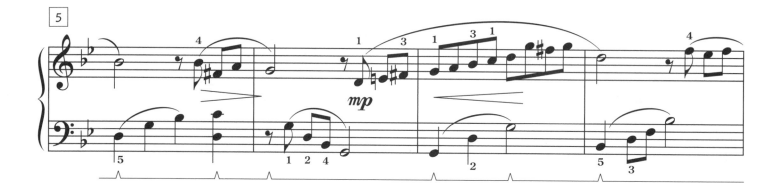

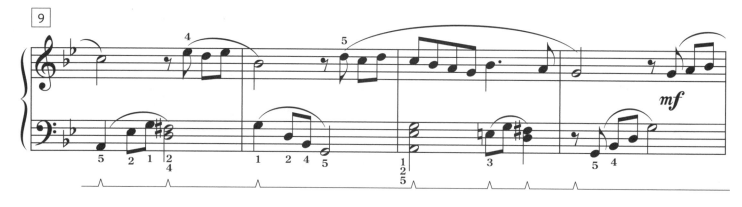

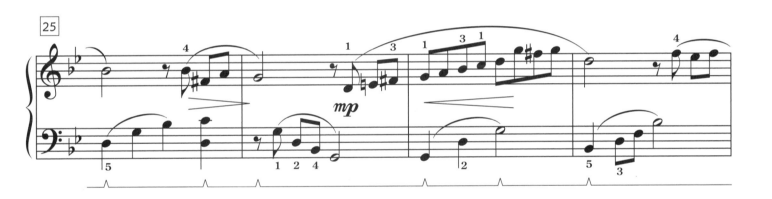

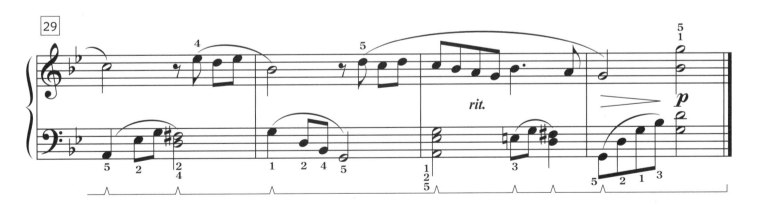

Premier Performer   *Listen for smooth pedal changes.*

Lesson Book: pages 46–47

Downtown
Jazz

CD 29/30 GM 15

Premier Performer *Play in a relaxed and improvisatory style.*

List of Compositions

Note: *Each selection on the CD is performed twice. The first track number is a performance tempo. The second track number is a slower practice tempo.*

The publisher hereby grants the purchaser of this book permission to download the enclosed CD to an MP3 or digital player (such as an Apple iPod®) for personal practice and performance.

	CD Track	Page
Blues Toccata	23/24	24
Caprice	1/2	2
Climbing the Pyrenees	25/26	26
Downtown Jazz	29/30	30
Fifers, The	11/12	12
German Dance	13/14	14
June: Barcarolle	27/28	28
Little Etude	15/16	15
Minuetto	7/8	8
Missouri River Ballad	3/4	4
Soldier's March	17/18	16
Sonatina in C Major (Second Movement)	19/20	18
Sonatina in C Major (Third Movement)	21/22	20
Splash of Indigo, A	5/6	6
Watercolor Impressions	9/10	10

CD Performances by Scott Price